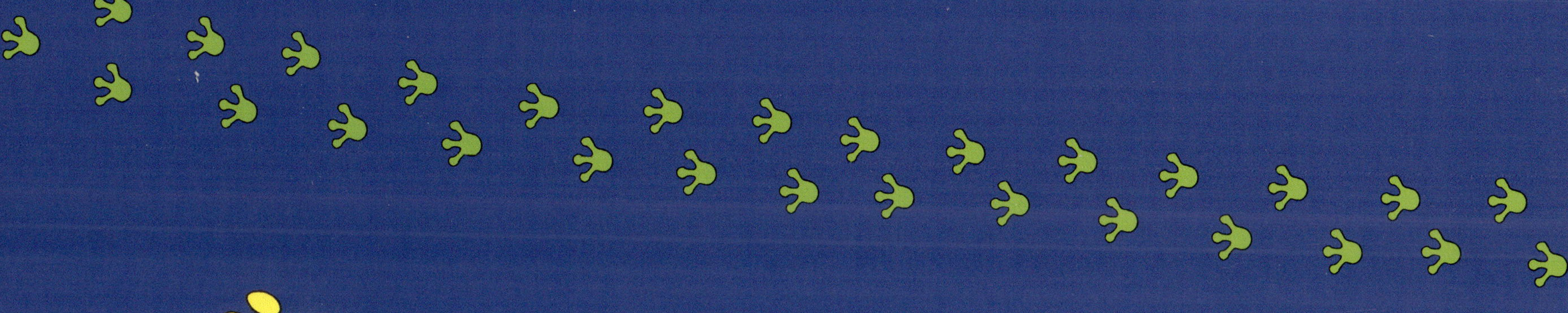

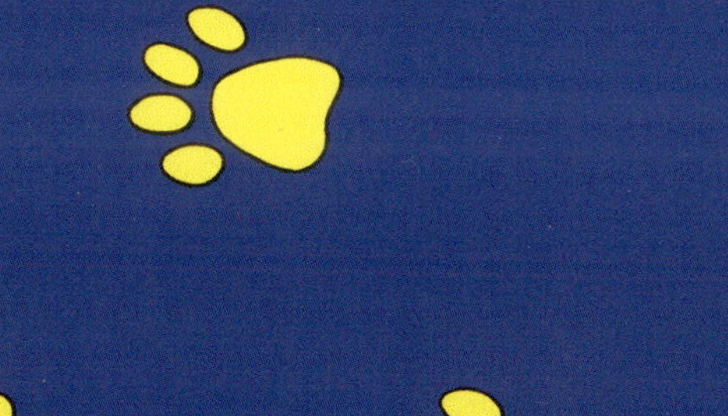

Enjoy!
Kaana

THE CAT AND THE GECKO

Every night when the lights went out, the gecko gave the cat a shout. "OK, my friend, are you ready to go? They're all asleep and they'll never know."

The cat gave a wink and nodded her head.
“Come on, let’s go while they’re all still in bed. An adventure awaits for us to see, not anyone else but just you and me.”

Up the hills and far away, they roamed through the fields
in the darkest of days.
They heard from friends of these long-haired foes,
who were ever so big they could bite off your nose!

Their hair was brown
down to their toes.

With spikes on their head –
for why, who knows?

Ten feet wide and
ten feet tall.

Oh, no! We're going to
look ever so small!

They reached the top and they heard a sound.
Quickly they scampered lower to the ground.
Could this be it - are the giants near?
For the frightening sound echoed ever so clear.

“Come on, let’s run. I don’t want to see the long-haired giants who are sure to eat me.”
Before they could blink they both froze, for leaning right over them was a BIG WET NOSE!

The cat looked up and the giant said, “Hello, what brings you here and why did you want to go?”

“The long-haired giants are what we came to see.”
“Can I just ask one question ...”

"ARE YOU GOING TO EAT ME?"

The giant gave an enormous laugh.
"Eat you?" he replied. "Don't be daft!"
"I'm just a Highland cow, who actually is kind.
Like a big gentle giant, if you don't mind."

I have brown hair
down to my toes.

I've two spikes on my head –
for why, do you know?

I am quite big –
pretty scary to some.

But if we become friends,
I promise we'll have fun!

“Why don’t you try me – come on, let’s go.
You just need to be brave, or you’ll never know.”
So they plucked up the courage and with one big jump,
they took off with the cow, with a stomp, stomp, stomp!

From that day on a friendship arose,
an unlikely one – whoever was to know
that a gecko, a cat and a Highland cow
were to become best friends together somehow.

So strange as it seems – they are an odd three,
but you don't always know who your friends will be.

So when that special someone comes and says hello,
an adventure could await you – you just never know!

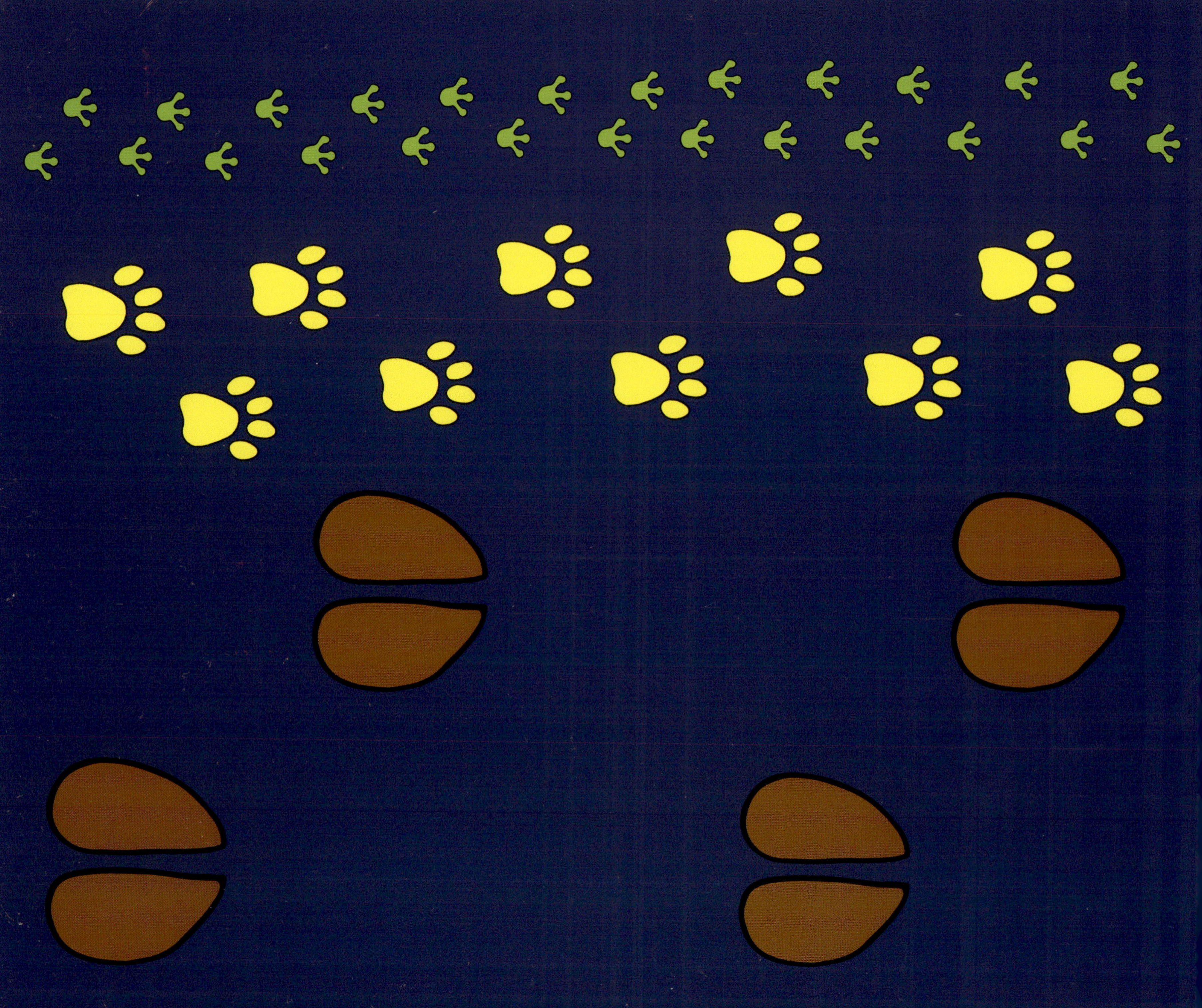